*Support
Our Troops*

Support Our Troops

Quotations on Patriotism and Prayer

Compiled by Eric Dinyer
Foreword by Carolyn Howard-Johnson

Andrews McMeel Publishing

Kansas City

Support Our Troops

05 06 07 08 09 SDB 10 9 8 7 6 5 4 3 2 1

ISBN-13: 978-0-7407-5564-4
ISBN-10: 0-7407-5564-1

Book design by Diane Marsh

ATTENTION: SCHOOLS AND BUSINESSES
Andrews McMeel books are available at quantity discounts with bulk purchase for educational, business, or sales promotional use. For information, please write to: Special Sales Department, Andrews McMeel Publishing, 4520 Main Street, Kansas City, Missouri 64111.

FOREWORD

I saw my grandson off to war . . .

My grandson. Heads for danger, heat, and sand. Alone.

—Carolyn Howard-Johnson, *Tracings*

That was the way I felt that day in the spring of 2004 as I watched my grandson graduate from boot camp.

My husband, a retired army reserve officer, and I had watched our young private on a field with hundreds of others, salute their flag, take their oaths. Fort Jackson, South Carolina. A hot, humid day. Travis's face now looked flat, pasted behind a window, an upside-down smiley pattern behind windows tinted khaki, his bus taking him away from me. I looked at the other graduates about to leave for assignments that would prepare them for Iraq. Some of these new soldiers were young, as I had imagined. Many were men, as I had expected. Others did not fit my preconceived notions of a newly minted soldier. Some were patriots in their thirties. Many were women. Many, both men and women, were kissing their own children good-bye. Each was giving up much but each was gaining something. Each was part of my new sense of patriotism, part of growing respect for our armed services.

I was impressed by the changes the military had already made in my grandson. He had lost weight. His muscles were taut. In his smile I saw a level of confidence I had not known before. There was a new vigor in the way he moved.

I was impressed by the sheer numbers graduating, my grandson's class multiplied by many. I realized how our nation needed them, how those already serving needed to be infused with these fresh, new, strong recruits.

I was impressed not by their bravery because I expected that, but by their intensity. Travis told me how much he had learned about dedication and responsibility in these past few weeks.

I was impressed by the prayers. "Bless you" was uttered as often as good-bye. I understood at a visceral level how prayers are not words but an internal longing; only a fraction of them reach our lips but all are as authentic as if uttered on bended knee.

FOREWORD

Since then, yellow ribbons sported around our nation—in our trees, tied to our mailboxes, placed on everything from car bumpers to students' backpacks—made me realize that Travis is not alone.

I can't say that these revelations made me less sad or less worried. They did, however, increase my pride, and give me courage (yes, bravery is required of military families, too), as the quotes in this book are designed to do. These soldiers have each other and they have the support of you and me. I am honored to be asked to share still more of these ribbons. They are, indeed, not only tokens of affection for our troops but also for the families who love them.

Blessings to you all,
Carolyn Howard-Johnson

He who lives without prayer, he who lives with little prayer, he who seldom reads the Word, and he who seldom looks up to heaven for a fresh influence from on high—he will be the man whose heart will become dry and barren.

—Charles Haddon Spurgeon

There are those, I know, who will say

that the liberation of humanity, the freedom

of man and mind, is nothing but a dream.

They are right. It is the American dream.

—Archibald MacLeish

The cement of this union is the heart-blood of every American.

—Thomas Jefferson

Remember that you can pray any time, anywhere. Washing dishes, digging ditches, working in the office, in the shop, on the athletic field, even in prison—you can pray and know God hears!

—Billy Graham

This nation will remain the land of the free only so long as it is the home of the brave.

—Elmer Davis

The stern hand of fate has scourged us to an elevation where we can see the great everlasting things that matter for a nation; the great peaks of honor we had forgotten—duty and patriotism, clad in glittering white; the great pinnacle of sacrifice pointing like a rugged finger to heaven.

—David Lloyd George

Prayer begins where human capacity ends.

—Marian Anderson

SOMETIMES PEOPLE CALL ME AN IDEALIST.

WELL, THAT IS THE WAY I KNOW I AM AN

AMERICAN. AMERICA IS THE ONLY IDEALISTIC

NATION IN THE WORLD.

—Woodrow Wilson

America is much more than a geographical fact.
It is a political and moral fact—the first community
in which men set out in principle to institutionalize
freedom, responsible government, and human equality.
—Adlai E. Stevenson

PRAYER REQUIRES MORE OF THE
HEART THAN THE TONGUE.
—Adam Clarke

Ours is the only country deliberately

PRAYER IS SPIRITUAL COMMU-NICATION BETWEEN MAN AND GOD, A TWO-WAY RELATIONSHIP IN WHICH MAN SHOULD NOT ONLY TALK TO GOD BUT ALSO LISTEN TO HIM. PRAYER TO GOD IS LIKE A CHILD'S CONVERSATION WITH HIS FATHER. IT IS NATURAL FOR A CHILD TO ASK HIS FATHER FOR THE THINGS HE NEEDS.

—Billy Graham

Oh, it's home again and home again, America for me!
I want a ship that's westward bound to plough the rolling sea
To the blessed land of room enough beyond the ocean bars,
Where the air is full of sunlight and the flag is full of stars.
—Henry Van Dyke

founded on a good idea.
—John Gunther

This, then, is the state of the union: free and restless, growing and full of hope. So it was in the beginning. So it shall always be, while God is willing, and we are strong enough to keep the faith.

—Lyndon B. Johnson

All I know is that when I pray, coincidences happen; and when I don't pray, they don't happen.

—Dan Hayes

It is the love of country that has lighted and that keeps glowing the holy fire of patriotism.

—J. Horace McFarland

The winds that blow through the wide sky in these mounts, the winds that sweep from Canada to Mexico, from the Pacific to the Atlantic—have always blown on free men.

—Franklin D. Roosevelt

Off with your hat, as the flag goes by!

And let the heart have its say;

you're man enough for a tear in your eye

that you will not wipe away.

—Henry Cuyler Bunner

Let EVERYONE TRY AND FIND THAT AS A RESULT OF DAILY PRAYER HE ADDS SOMETHING NEW TO HIS LIFE, SOMETHING WITH WHICH NOTHING CAN BE COMPARED.

—Mahatma Gandhi

I wish that every human life might be pure transparent freedom.

—Simone de Beauvoir

Our country is not the only thing to which we owe our allegiance. It is also owed to justice and to humanity. Patriotism consists not in waving the flag, but in striving that our country shall be righteous as well as strong.

—James Bryce

Prayer is not eloquence, but earnestness; not the definition of helplessness, but the feeling of it; not figures of speech, but earnestness of soul.

—Hannah More

Those who won our *independence*
believed *liberty* to be the secret of happiness
and *courage* to be the secret of liberty.

—Louis D. Brandeis

Prayer is not only asking, but an

attitude of mind which produces the atmosphere

in which asking is perfectly natural.

—Oswald Chambers

 I think there is one higher
office than president and I would
call that patriot.

—Gary Hart

*I*ntellectually I know that America is no better than any other country; emotionally I know she is better than every other country.

—Sinclair Lewis

Throughout our history, Americans of faith have always turned to prayer—for wisdom, prayer for resolve, prayers for compassion and strength, prayers for commitment to justice and for a spirit of forgiveness.

—George W. Bush

We can't all be Washingtons, but we can all be patriots.

—Charles F. Browne

This is America . . .
we can do anything here!

—*Ted Turner*

I am a great believer in luck,
and I find that the harder I work
the more luck I have.

—Thomas Jefferson

SO I TELL YOU, WHATEVER YOU ASK FOR

IN PRAYER, BELIEVE THAT YOU HAVE

RECEIVED IT, AND IT WILL BE YOURS.

—Matthew 21:22

LOVE YOUR COUNTRY. Your country is the land where your parents sleep, where is spoken that language in which the chosen of your heart, blushing, whispered the first word of love; it is the home that God has given you that by striving to perfect yourselves therein you may prepare to ascend to him.

—Giuseppe Mazzini

We may pray most when we say least, and we may pray least when we say most.

—St. Augustine of Hippo

If our country is worth dying for in time of war let us resolve that it is truly worth living for in time of peace.

—Hamilton Fish

What do we mean by patriotism in the context of our times? I venture to suggest that what we mean is a sense of national responsibility . . . a patriotism which is not short, frenzied outbursts of emotion, but the tranquil and steady dedication of a lifetime.

—Adlai E. Stevenson

If the only prayer you said in your whole life was, *"thank you,"* that would suffice.

—Meister Eckhart

I was *born* an American;

I will *live* an American;

I shall *die* an American!

—Daniel Webster, July 1850 speech

A moment comes, which comes but rarely

in history, when we step out from the old to the

new, when an age ends, and when the sound of a

nation, long suppressed, finds utterance.

—Jawaharlal Nehru

Seven days without prayer makes one weak.
—Allen E. Bartlett

Every good citizen makes his country's honor his own, and cherishes it not only as precious but as sacred. He is willing to risk his life in its defense and is conscious that he gains protection while he gives it.
—Andrew Jackson

A nation reveals itself not only by the men it produces but also by the men it honors, the men it remembers.

—John F. Kennedy

DO NOT MAKE PRAYER A MONOLOGUE—MAKE IT A CONVERSATION.
—Author unknown

A man's country is not a certain area of land, of mountains, rivers, and woods, but it is a principle; and patriotism is loyalty to that principle.
—George William Curtis

Patriotism is
just loyalty to friends,
people, families.

—*Robert Santos*

MEN MAY SPURN OUR APPEALS, reject our message, oppose our arguments, despise our persons, but they are helpless against our prayers.

—J. Sidlow Baxter

Our country is not the only thing to which we owe our allegiance. It is also owed to justice and to humanity. Patriotism consists not in waving the flag, but in striving that our country shall be righteous as well as strong.

—James Bryce

This land is your land, this land is my land,
from California to the New York Island.
From the redwood forest to the Gulf Stream waters,
this land was made for you and me.

—Woody Guthrie

To get nations back on their feet, we must first get down on our knees.

—Billy Graham

OUR NATION—THIS GENERATION—will lift a dark threat of violence from our people and our future. We will rally the world to this cause by our efforts, by our courage. We will not tire, we will not falter, and we will not fail.

—George W. Bush

This massive attack was intended to break our spirit.
It has not done that.
It has made us stronger, more determined,
and more resolved.

—Rudolph Giuliani

Prayer should be the key of the day
and the lock of the night.

—Charles Haddon Spurgeon

I believe it is the duty of every

man to act as though the fate of the world

depends on them. Surely no one man can do it

all. But, one man *can* make a difference.

—Hyman Rickover

*S*ince America's founding, prayer has reassured us that the hand of God is guiding the affairs of this nation. We have never asserted a special claim on His favor, yet we've always believed in God's presence in our lives. This has always been true. Prayer has comforted people in grief. Prayer has served as a unifying factor in our nation. Prayer gives us strength for the journey ahead.

—George W. Bush

Courage is the price that life exacts
for granting peace with yourself.

—*Amelia Earhart*

*T*AKE TIME TO DELIBERATE; BUT WHEN THE TIME FOR ACTION ARRIVES, STOP THINKING AND GO IN.

—Andrew Jackson

Peace is the highest aspiration of the

American People. We will negotiate for it, sacrifice

for it; we will never surrender for it, now or ever.

—Ronald. W. Reagan

Sometimes the most important thing in a
whole day is the rest we take between two
deep breaths, or the turning inwards in
prayer for five short minutes.

—Etty Hillesum

Although the world is full of suffering,
it is full also of the overcoming of it.

—Helen Keller

Prayer is the voice of faith.
—William Van Horne

Yet DESPITE THE QUESTIONS WE ALL ARE ASKING, REGARDLESS OF THE FEARS WE MAY BE EXPERIENCING, ONE FACT IS CLEAR: WE WILL PULL TOGETHER AS A NATION DURING THIS TIME OF CRISIS.
—Jimmy Carter

LIBERTY IS A THING OF THE SPIRIT— to be free to worship, to think, to hold opinions, and to speak without fear—free to challenge wrong and oppression with surety of justice.
—Herbert Hoover

Responding to challenge is one of democracy's greatest strengths.
—Neil Armstrong

I BELIEVE IN PRAYER. It's the best way
we have to draw strength from heaven.
—Josephine Baker

THOSE WHO EXPECT TO REAP THE
BLESSINGS OF FREEDOM, MUST, LIKE MEN,
UNDERGO THE FATIGUES OF SUPPORTING IT.
—Thomas Paine

Yours the message cheering
That the time is nearing
Which will see
All men free,
Tyrants disappearing.
—"Rock of Ages," a Chanukah hymn

*Do what you can, with what you have,
where you are.*
—Theodore Roosevelt

When you get in a tight place and everything goes against you, till it seems you could not hold on a minute longer, never give up then, for that is just the place and time that the tide will turn.

—Harriet Beecher Stowe

The things that the flag stands for were created by the experiences of a great people. Everything that it stands for was written by their lives. The flag is the embodiment, not of sentiment, but of history.

—Woodrow Wilson

BE JOYFUL IN HOPE, PATIENT IN AFFLICTION, FAITHFUL IN PRAYER.

—Romans 12:12

*G*od bless America, land that I love,
Stand beside her and guide her
Through the night with a light from above.
From the mountains, to the prairies,
To the oceans white with foam, God bless America,
My home sweet home.

—Irving Berlin

My basic principle is that you don't make decisions

because they are easy; you don't make them because

they are cheap; you don't make them because they are

popular; you make them because they are right.

—Theodore Hesburgh

Pursuing prayer is prayer on a mission.
It is diligent, fervent, constant, persevering,
determined, and convinced.

—David Bryant

The power of prayer

is like turning on a light as it illuminates God's purpose for our lives. There is no greater connection to knowing His will other than the word.

—Thomas Kinkade

Those who deny freedom

to others deserve it not for

themselves, and, under a just

God, cannot long retain it.

—Abraham Lincoln

Freedom lies in being bold.
—Robert Frost

If there is righteousness in the *heart*, there will be beauty in the character. If there is *beauty* in the character, there will be harmony in the home. If there is *harmony* in the home, there will be order in the nation. When there is *order* in the nation, there will be *peace* in the world.

—Chinese proverb

The old ideas are new again because they are not old, they are timeless: duty, sacrifice, commitment, and a patriotism that finds its expression in taking part and pitching in.

—George Bush

YOU CAN DO MORE THAN PRAY AFTER YOU'VE PRAYED, BUT YOU CANNOT DO MORE THAN PRAY UNTIL YOU HAVE PRAYED.

—Author unknown

Prayer does not equip us
for the greater work,
prayer is the greater work.

—*Oswald Chambers*

Do not pray for easy lives. Pray to be stronger men. Do not pray for tasks commensurate with your strength. Pray for strength commensurate with your tasks.

—Author unknown

AMERICA! AMERICA!

God shed His grace on thee,

And crown thy good with brotherhood

From sea to shining sea!

—Katherine Lee Bates

National honor is national property of the highest value.
— James Monroe, first inaugural address,
March 4, 1817

Prayer is not a substitute for work, thinking, watching, suffering, or giving; prayer is a support for all other efforts.
—Adam Clarke

When an American says that he loves his country, he means not only that he loves the New England hills, the prairies glistening in the sun, the wide and rising plains, the great mountains, and the sea. He means that he loves an inner air, an inner light in which freedom lives and in which a man can draw the breath of self-respect.
—Adlai E. Stevenson

And so I want to thank you for your prayers. I want to thank you for what you do for our nation. I want to thank you for your good works. I want to thank you for helping change America one heart, one soul, one conscience at a time.

—George W. Bush

MAY THE SUN IN HIS COURSE

VISIT NO LAND MORE FREE, MORE

HAPPY, MORE LOVELY, THAN THIS

OUR OWN COUNTRY!

—Daniel Webster

The happy ending is our national belief.

—Mary McCarthy

*He who fails to pray does not cheat God.
He cheats himself.*

—George Failing

IT IS AN AMAZING
COINCIDENCE THAT
THE WORD AMERICAN
ENDS IN *CAN*.

—American saying

I (RE: GENERAL STONEWALL JACKSON, RECOUNTED
TO CHAPLAIN WILLIAM W. BENNETT)

I saw something today which affected me more than anything I ever saw or read on religion. While the battle was raging and the bullets were flying, Jackson rode by, calm as if he were at home, but his head was raised toward heaven, and his lips were moving evidently in prayer.

—William Federer

If you take advantage of everything America has to offer, there's nothing you can't accomplish.

—Geraldine Ferraro

Countless people pray far more than they know. Often they have such a "stained-glass" image of prayer that they fail to recognize what they are experiencing as prayer and so condemn themselves for not praying.

—Richard J. Foster

I like to see a man proud of the place in which he lives. I like to see a man live so that his place will be proud of him.

—Abraham Lincoln

Democracy is a small hard core of common agreement, surrounded by a rich variety of individual differences.

—James Bryant Conant

Prayer is nothing else than a sense of God's presence.

—*Brother Lawrence*

So let me assert my firm belief that the only thing we have to fear is fear itself.

—Franklin D. Roosevelt

IF WE WOULD TALK LESS AND PRAY MORE ABOUT THEM, THINGS WOULD BE BETTER THAN THEY ARE IN THE WORLD; AT LEAST, WE SHOULD BE BETTER ENABLED TO BEAR THEM.

—John Owen

I work the ropelines a lot, and people say, "Mr. President, I pray for you and your family." I turn to them, I look them in the eye, and say, that's the greatest gift you can give. That's the greatest gift you can give. I mean it with all sincerity.

—George W. Bush

THE GREATEST TRAGEDY OF LIFE
IS NOT UNANSWERED PRAYER,
BUT UN-OFFERED PRAYER.

—F. B. Meyer

The true test of civilization is—not the census, not the size of the cities, nor the crops—no, but the kind of man the country turns out.

—Ralph Waldo Emerson

More tears are shed over answered prayers than unanswered ones.

—Mother Teresa

If your day is hemmed in with prayer, it is less likely to come unraveled.
—Author unknown

What light is to the eyes—what air is to the lungs—what love is to the heart, liberty is to the soul of man . . .

—Robert Ingersoll

A GOOD COUNTRY SONG taps into strong undercurrents of family, faith, and patriotism.
—George W. Bush

PATRIOTISM IS VOLUNTARY. IT IS A FEELING OF LOYALTY AND ALLEGIANCE THAT IS THE RESULT OF KNOWLEDGE AND BELIEF. A PATRIOT SHOWS THEIR PATRIOTISM THROUGH THEIR ACTIONS, BY THEIR CHOICE.
—Jesse Ventura

The great people of the earth today are the people who pray, [not] those who talk about prayer . . . but I mean those who take time and pray.

—S. D. Gordon

PATRIOTISM is easy to understand in America—it means looking out for yourself by looking out for your country.

—Calvin Coolidge

ASK NOT WHAT YOUR COUNTRY CAN DO FOR YOU, BUT WHAT YOU CAN DO FOR YOUR COUNTRY.

—John F. Kennedy

I believe in America because we have great

dreams—and because we have the opportunity

to make those dreams come true.

—Wendell L. Wilkie

America is another name for opportunity.
Our whole history appears like a last effort of
divine providence on behalf of the human race.
—Ralph Waldo Emerson

Injustice anywhere is a threat
to justice everywhere.
—Martin Luther King Jr.

Prayer is not asking.

OUR GREAT MODERN REPUBLIC. May those who seek the blessings of its institutions and the protection of its flag remember the obligations they impose.

—Ulysses S. Grant

THE GREATEST GIFT WE CAN GIVE TO OTHERS IS OUR PRAYERS.

—Marian Anderson

*L*et every nation know, whether it wishes us well

or ill, that we shall pay any price, bear any burden,

meet any hardship, support any friend, oppose any foe,

in order to assure the survival and success of liberty.

—John F. Kennedy

It is a language of the soul.
—*Mahatma Gandhi*

To pray well is the better half of study.

—Martin Luther King Jr.

My God! How little do my countrymen know what precious blessings they are in possession of, and which no other people on earth enjoy!
—Thomas Jefferson

More things are wrought by prayer than this world dreams of.
—Alfred, Lord Tennyson

Then conquer we must, when our cause it is just,
And this be our motto: "In God is our trust!"
And the star-spangled banner in triumph shall wave
O'er the land of the free and the home of the brave.
—Francis Scott Key

Work should be for all of us a word as

honorable and appealing as *patriotism*.

—Dwight D. Eisenhower

*M*ay God give you . . .

For every storm a rainbow, for every tear a smile,

for every care a promise and a blessing in each trial.

For every problem life sends, a faithful friend to share,

for every sigh a sweet song and an answer for each prayer.

—Irish blessing

I have never advocated war except
as a means of peace.

—Ulysses S. Grant

Sometimes the *answer* to prayer

is not that it changes *life*, but

that it changes *you*.

—James Dillet Freeman

Justice delayed is
democracy denied.
—*Robert F. Kennedy*

IF YOU ARE ASHAMED TO STAND BY

YOUR COLORS, YOU HAD BETTER

SEEK ANOTHER FLAG.

—Author unknown